ON CIVILITY:
RESTORATIVE REFLECTIONS

John-Robert Curtin, Ph.D.

On Civility: Restorative Reflections
By John-Robert Curtin, Ph.D.

Published by Old Stone Press
an imprint of J. H. Clark & Associates, Inc.
Louisville, Kentucky 40207 USA

www.oldstonepress.com

© 2020, John-Robert Curtin, Ph.D.
All rights reserved.

This book may not be reproduced in whole or in part without written permission from the publisher, Old Stone Press, or from the author, John-Robert Curtin, Ph.D., except by a reviewer who may quote brief passages in a review; nor any part of this book be reproduced, stored in a retrieval system, or transmitted in any form or by any means, electronic, mechanical photocopying, audio recording or other recording, without written permission from publisher or author.

Book design: Ying Kit Chan
Photographs & Illustrations: Ying Kit Chan

For information about special discounts for bulk purchases or autographed copies of this book, please contact J. H. Clark, Old Stone Press at john@oldstonepress.com or the author John-Robert Curtin, Ph.D., 4Civility at jr@4civility.org

On Civility: Restorative Reflections
By John-Robert Curtin, Ph.D.

Library of Congress Control Number: 2020901656

ISBN: 978-1-938462-42-9 (print)
ISBN: 978-1-938462-43-6 (eBook)

Published in USA

"Conflict is not the problem; conflict is the messenger."

Tony Belak, Esquire, Mediator, Ombuds

To

Frederick Smock, Kentucky State Poet Laureate 2017-2018, who encouraged me to publish and share this work outside of my classroom.

CONTENTS

1	ON ASSUMPTIONS
4	ON CIRCLES
7	ON DESTINY
12	ON ENDING OUR CONFLICT WITH A COMMON STORY
15	ON LISTENING: A GIFT OF COMPASSION
19	ON LISTENING TO UNDERSTAND
21	ON LOVE IS GOD
23	ON RESTORATIVE PRACTICES
28	ON THE SEVEN STATES OF OUR PERSONAL BEING
29	I. ON THE MENTAL STATE OF BEING
31	II. ON THE EMOTIONAL STATE OF BEING
35	III. ON THE PHYSICAL STATE OF BEING
37	IV. ON THE TRANSPERSONAL STATE OF BEING
39	V. ON THE VALUES STATE OF BEING
41	VI. ON THE ETHICAL STATE OF BEING
43	VII. ON THE HISTORICAL AND INHERITED STATE OF BEING
47	ON THE IMPORTANCE OF THE STORY
51	ON THE LOSS OF OUR DIGNITY
55	ON BEING TRUMPED OR CHUMPED
57	ON WORKPLACE INCIVILITY
61	ON UNDERSTANDING OUR WORDS
63	ON TRUST, DISTRUST, AND THE SPACE BETWEEN
66	ON IF YOU WANT TO KEEP IT, GIVE IT AWAY
69	ON HOPE
71	ON THE IMPORTANCE OF FEELINGS
73	ON THE QUESTION OF LIFE
75	ON LEADING BY EXAMPLE
79	ON ARE YOU DISPOSABLE; ARE OTHERS?

ON ASSUMPTIONS

Eight-five percent of my assumptions are incorrect.
I am not sure about the other fifteen percent.
Am I the only one who knows about wrong assumptions?
Do most people just go with their gut, as I once did?

Withholding judgment until one tests assumptions is hard work,
it requires discipline, self-doubt, and compassion.
It is not for the faint of heart.
It is much easier to simply be the judge, jury and executioner.

Life is so much simpler when one is right all the time,
regardless of reality, or truth. But what is true?
If my assumptions are wrong 85% of the time how
do I know truth, do I ever know what is true?

ON CIRCLES

Circles, a universal connector, a foundation for equality,
a joiner of people, and a catalyst for conversation.
Circles began as an ancient custom which fostered
listening and understanding. Discussion circles,
which appear to come from this ancient
wisdom, are really an outgrowth of our ancestors'
practical solution for survival. Early families, tribes, and clans
used circles for light, for heat, for protection from beasts,
and for cooking. The results were remarkably wise,
for the circles accomplished the practical needs, but
almost by accident created a level platform for civil
discussion, storytelling, sharing, listening, and understanding.

Their circles gave them a structure to relate as equals.
They allowed for an equality among groups
that remained equal until the beginning of the
dominator society, when one or more
members of the group decided that they were more equal
than the others and found ways to elevate themselves
above the group. It wasn't long before that elevation was

symbolized by raising the sitting position of the new leader, and adorning their status with what we would now refer to as 'bling.'

We continued to use circles to gather, but we began referring to them as campfires. We have always loved campfires. We have used them often for some of the same reasons our forebears used them. We love the stories and the camaraderie at campfires, and we especially love the s'mores, but we are only now, with the revival of restorative practices, learning to use circles for more than the campfire, for the more human and important leveling of our humanity, equality, and understanding. We are learning to use circles to heal, to listen to each other, to connect our humanity, and to restore our relationships.

ON DESTINY

Let your thoughts be positive for they will become your words.
Let your words be positive for they will become your actions.
Let your actions be positive for they will become your values.
Let your values be positive for they will become your destiny.
                                             Mahatma Gandhi

What is my destiny? It will be mine, I will have earned it, I deserve it, no matter what it turns out to be. I will have worked on it for many years. I can change the course if I desire, but it will not be easy. Thoughts, words, actions, and values are not readily redirected. They leave a trail, a legacy, a pattern, and a history. They will always be part of my destiny even if I can alter each with new insight, new thoughts, new words, and new deeds. I will always own those that I have embraced in the past.

I must carry them into the future even if I wish to
forsake my old ways, I will still own them. I can only
move in a new direction by owning up to the honesty
of accepting my past. If the truth can set one free,
that freedom can only come with the acceptance of the past
and the reckoning of that acceptance. I cannot change
my spots, but I can acknowledge the blemishes, the
warts, and the scars, mine and the others I have
created. They will always be there for me and
others to see. If I wish to change I must build on the past,
through honesty, acknowledgement, and reflection.

My future will depend on my honestly changing my thoughts, words, and values. I can embrace new patterns if I take positive steps in the correction each hour of each day. I cannot dwell on the past except in understanding its role in my history, and its constant pressure to return to old ways. If I can truly embrace a new direction while remembering my past failures, I may have a chance at a new future. It is what Dr. William Glasser preached with Reality Therapy. If I can make small steps in the right direction while remembering why I made those bad decisions in the past, I can use the past as a foundation for a new beginning, a new reality and perhaps a new destiny. If I do that by conscious choice and then continue that new path, constantly taking small steps to reinforce my journey, I may find a new self, one that not only changes me but all those that I touch. It will be my destiny.

ON ENDING OUR CONFLICT WITH A COMMON STORY

When we are in conflict…I have a story, you have a story. I know my story is correct, true and honest. You not only believe I am wrong, but that my story is inaccurate, maybe false, surely a prevarication.

How can it be otherwise? Since you have your own true story, that frankly, I don't like, don't believe, and am not ready to hear again. We can go on, comfortable in our own stories, and uncomfortable with each other for the rest of our lives. And in doing so deny each other's story again and again. But what if by some miracle or some magical process we actually stop and listen to each other?

And in the process, we begin to
listen to understand, not to respond
and amazingly, we begin to
sense how each of our stories has affected our
emotions, our assumptions, and
our temperament. Perhaps
as I finally hear your story and
learn the emotions behind your story,
you might hear mine and learn my
feelings. Remarkably, a new common story will
emerge. As we both embrace
our new shared common story we
might actually embrace each other. At
least we will shake hands. It's a good start.

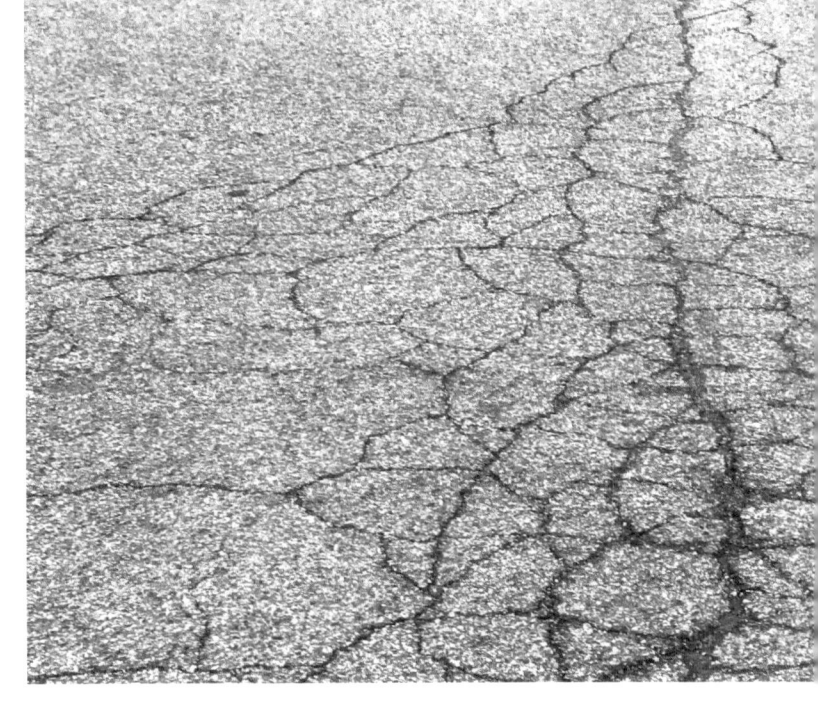

ON LISTENING: A GIFT OF COMPASSION

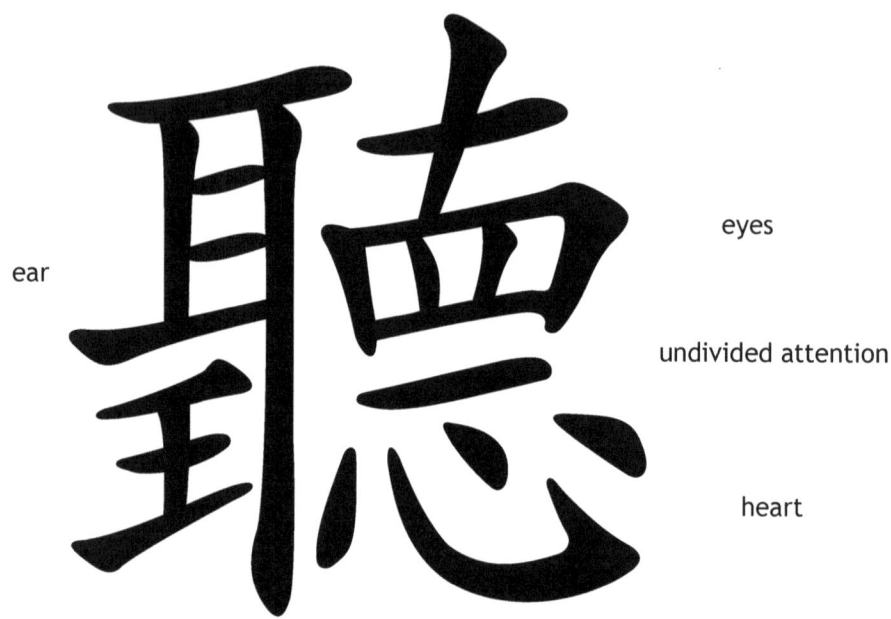

Chinese character for the verb "to listen"

Listen with your eyes, your mind, your compassion,
…… not just your ears. Listen to understand,
not to respond. There will be ample time
to respond once you understand and the speaker
senses you understand. And because you now
understand your response can be one of
compassion demonstrating your full attention,
complete with open ended questions and
delivered with an affirming tone and open body language.

Listening to understand is a gift that you can bestow on others while you receive a tremendous return on investment. I learn very little when I am listening to respond and at best, I only amplify my own ignorance as I convince myself of my own importance. When I listen to understand whole new vistas open before my eyes and I engage in learning.

Open ended questions continue the learning phenomenon as deeper understanding creeps into my consciousness. It is a gift: a gift to me, a sharing of humanity, a reaffirmation of human connection, an ancient adaptation that elevated human beings to find connections, humanity, and survival. Listening to understand is an act that defines love of life.

ON LISTENING TO UNDERSTAND

It's amazing what you hear when you listen.
                                    Yogi Berra

"Do you hear what I hear; do you see what I see?"
Is this only Christmas music or can we actually
hear and see what others see? Is it possible?
What does it take; is it training, hard work,
both or some supernatural gift?

The real gift comes through
abandoning listening to respond
and learning to listen to understand.
I learn very little when my lips are moving, except
perhaps what I already know. How good is that,
who does it help, unless it is coupled with sharing?
When I listen to understand, I begin to make a human
connection. A connection which is quickly lost
when I interrupt. If my advice is so valuable
why do I not take it myself? Why should you
listen when I talk, what is in it for you?

If I try to understand you, your thoughts can
improve mine and your chance to be truly heard
might be a completely new experience for us both.
We both might learn, we might both benefit;
what a novel idea. Active listening is a gift
of compassion. You can only keep
compassion by giving it away.
You cannot hoard compassion, you cannot
stockpile it to save it for a rainy day.
You must actively and purposely give it away
if you want any chance of keeping some for yourself.

ON LOVE IS GOD

Love is the greatest force in the universe. It is the heartbeat of the moral cosmos. He who loves is a participant in the being of God.

Dr. Martin Luther King Jr.

Love is all powerful, all giving;

a force that must be felt,

experienced, and implemented.

Pure love is more precious than gold

and cannot be given away selectively.

It must be given unconditionally, without

motive or a desire for a return on

investment. It is a force, perhaps the

most powerful of all forces.

Love can build, it can defeat hate,
insincerity, ambiguity, and
greed. We can learn to love,
just as we have learned to hate. Once
learned we must practice, question,
relearn, and adjust to how the
force will engulf us and those we touch.
It is not an easy road but we might
find it more perfect than the
road we usually take. Once taken
there is no turning back, no backtracking,
rerouting, for love is god. Love is creationism
at its best.

ON RESTORATIVE PRACTICES

Restorative Practices searches for normalcy, it searches for courageous conversations, it seeks to foster communications between human beings in a crude but essential quest for understanding of needs, normalcy, interest, and of misdeeds. Why is that so hard? Will we ever get it right? How can a species built for cooperation find so many ways to be uncooperative?

Restorative Practices finds its roots in restorative justice, an ancient practice from our days in small clans, tribes, and families. What began as a struggle for survival when we needed everyone for our groups' survival. When for our survival, we had to find a way for our group to protect and restore victims, reintegrate offenders back to a productive relationship with our tribe, in a community setting involving bystanders directly in the process of assisting both victims and offenders.

It was at a time when we as humans did not have the luxury of treating other humans as disposable, we needed everyone, if we were to survive. Why is today different? Why do we now see other humans as disposable? How can we? What have we wasted, what have we lost, and who are we to choose who survives? We need to return to an understanding of human value, of human connection, and human worth. We need to adopt Restorative Practices in every phase of our lives, home, community, work, and international relations if we are to remain human and to survive in a way that continues to connect. Restorative Practices provides Truth with Compassion and returns us to our most basic definition of humanity.

ON THE SEVEN STATES OF OUR PERSONAL BEING

The amount of positive control one has with each of the seven states is a measure of positive stability. When one does not have positive control/stability over one or more of the seven states, there is a tendency to compensate for the lack of control, typically with negative thoughts, actions, and deeds. Control is then established through conscious or unconscious rationalization as justification for negative behavior.

I.

On the Mental State of Being

Stability, intelligence, competency and the control one has
over one's mental state will determine social and emotional
interaction and connection. Mental control will affect
emotional, spiritual, and cultural intelligence.
Lacking mental control forces efforts
to compensate, often through negative thoughts, actions,
and deeds. The basic need for control is common to all
human beings. Attempts to control one's mental
state of being can be maddening, hallucinating, irrational,
and destructive.

Positive attempts to control are difficult at best,
and almost impossible to undertake alone.
The sense of losing one's mind
is a direct reaction to the struggle to find control.
Negative control is much easier to achieve
and can be aided in the struggle by
conscious and unconscious rationality
resulting in justification for negative
and destructive behavior. The road to insanity
is paved with rationality, fantasy, and paranoia.

For all human beings, the struggle for control can be elusive, demanding, frustrating, depressing, and necessitates some periods of darkness. It can become a personal forty days in the wilderness, alone, introspective, and emotional. Emerging intact, if possible, will contribute to a renewed sense of connection to oneself and to others. Not emerging leads to insanity, loneliness, and isolation. Humans are meant to be connected, connected to others and to oneself. Positive connections determine one's mental state of being.

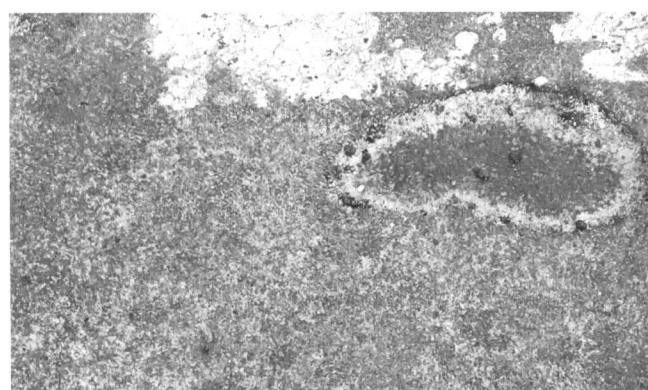

II.

On the Emotional State of Being

Emotional orientation and emotional control are
integral to rational stability. Understanding our own
emotions combined with sensing the emotions of others is
often referred to as emotional intelligence (EQ) and is a key
component for stable connections. EQ is believed to be more
important to our individual development and overall
success than IQ. EQ connects each of us with ourselves
and others. EQ fosters positive relationships
and understanding. It stabilizes relationships and
allows for empathy and lays the ground work
for compassion.

When we are unable to control our emotions
we tend to react before we think. Our actions
are almost always negative, sometimes verbally, sometimes
physically. But always in ways that can be destructive
to ourselves and to others. If we are somewhat rational
we find ourselves apologizing way too often.
When we are driven by our emotions and

we are unable to control them we are on a collision course with inappropriate behavior, broken relationships, negativity, and loneliness. It is possible to learn to control our emotions. Often that is what children learn as they mature. For adults outside coaching may help, but self-coaching is difficult and almost impossible.

Stress can readily reduce our emotional control and learning to reduce stress can be a factor in regaining control. Deep breathing and meditation can also help to reduce stress and gain emotional control, but the severely out-of-control may need professional help to obtain regular control and thereby move to a level of stability.

III.
On the Physical State of Being

Our physical state of being controls our mobility,
our strength, and our physical fitness.
A healthy physical body needs a coupling
with a healthy mind to reach its potential.
A positive or negative reaction
to our own physical state, including any
disabilities or frailties, and the
reaction of others toward our state
can be a force for our empowerment or
continued frustration.

Controlling the physical state of being
is not always possible, but presenting
a positive attitude is not only possible,
but essential for well-being. Adapting
to our physical state of being with
an attitude toward improvement or
positively accommodating for
freedom and independence is
empowering. Reacting negatively
is destructive, crippling, and powerless.

IV.

On the Transpersonal State of Being

How we see others and how we perceive
they see us is a form of emotional intelligence
that can be positive and enlightening, or
fraught with wrongful assumptions,
mischaracterizations, and dislike. Without
positive control of our transpersonal being
we will tend to gain control through
negative responses, judgmental decisions,
and rudeness. Our failure to understand,
or our misconceptions, foster anger
and relationship destroying behavior.

Strong control of our transpersonal being allows for understanding, connections, and compassion, but only if we have transpersonal control and compassion for our self can we have compassion for others. Without transpersonal control and self-compassion, we are left with envy, jealousy, and dysfunction.

V.

On the Values State of Being

Personal values reflect one's concept
of morality, truth, right, and wrong. They
are a compass heading, a safe path,
a warm comfortable place of being.
They can also be a place of great conflict
since values like morals are contextual
and are learned in our separate tribes.

A strong value state of being can
allow us to understand
the values of others without revulsion,
prejudice, and moral judgment.
We can see differences between
the values of their and our tribe.
It can keep us from making moral
comparisons. Strong control of
our value state of being recognizes
differences as differences and not
immoral flaws that must be corrected
through power, law, or coercion.

Strong control of our value state
can foster dialog and debate, but
only if we listen can we learn and
understand another tribe's values
and how they relate to our own.

VI.
On the Ethical State of Being

Our personal ethics and our ability to recognize and understand the ethics of others are indicators of our ethical state of being. An ability to determine and live by our own ethical code is reflected through our consistency, honesty, and forthrightness. It is the basis of our personal compass and our lifetime sense of integrity.

Loss of ethical control is the breeding ground of sociopathic behavior. The total lack of ethical control destroys relationships, lives, and communities. Even the temporary loss of ethical control can mean a lifetime of misery for individuals, communities, and nations.

Ethical control is not only doing what is right when no one can see you, but is doing what is right when everyone can see you. Your very public display of ethical control can have a moralizing effect on negative situations and show compassion and respect for others when you publicly stand and are counted, for right, rights, and responsibility.

VII.

On the Historical and Inherited State of Being

A person has no ability to determine their historical and inherited background, but they do have the ability to not let the inheritance control their lives to a point that they do damage to others and their communities. Even though they might have won the lucky sperm lottery they never bought the ticket, it was purchased for them.

The fact that a person grew up with
a sense of privileged entitlement does not
mean they are special. In fact, if they will accept it,
it may mean that they have a special responsibility
for those who are not as fortunate.
For them the task is to learn to understand
others and learn to practice compassion.
They need to know they may not have the ability
to change the wind, but they can adjust the sails
and steer toward a compassionate harbor.
Their resilience to not submit to adopting
learned or inherited prejudices and hatred
can be the mark of true control.

For those who inherited repression and discrimination
control may mean finding inner joy and
building on strength and will to rise above
the depths that society has allocated
to them. The task is not to allow the moral
failures of others to continue to trample
their spirit or define them as inferior.
It is a difficult journey, often begun
without tools, resources, or basic needs.
The journey becomes even more difficult
if anger, bitterness, and hatred are carried
on the path. The ability to recognize
the right to have those negative tools,
but to not carry them or use them
along the journey is a true
measure of control of the inherited state of being.

ON THE IMPORTANCE OF THE STORY

We learn from stories, we always have. Perhaps,
it is what makes us humans and distinguishes
us from other life forms. We learn from stories, we
always have, we pass them through generations, we
embrace them, we convert them, we sometimes corrupt
them, and we believe them to be true.
But what is true, how can we know truth,
except from other stories? Stories, when
true, become facts. But facts can be
meaningless without stories, without context, without
connection. Our connections come from stories,
not facts. When we have separate, disconnected stories
we create, if not careful, conflict,
resentment, distrust, and even disdain.

It is only when we hear and share our separate stories that we have a chance of creating a more accurate common story. As we gravitate to our new common story we may find a new connection, an understanding, a new beginning. We must share our stories, it is what makes us human, but we cannot share them if we do not hear each other. We cannot hear each other unless we listen; listen with our eyes, our hearts, and our compassion. Only then can we connect and connection is everything, it is the only thing worth having. It's what makes us human.

ON THE LOSS OF OUR DIGNITY

When did we as rational human beings decide that some
other human beings were disposable? We do that, do we not?
For how long have we made these irrational decisions?
Who does it benefit? Certainly, not mankind
since in our early days, when we existed in
small clans, tribes, and families, we understood that we needed
all members of our group for our mutual survival.
We needed each of our members to survive and contribute,
for our own survival. We struggled to find ways to support
those that were offended, but also to find meaningful
ways for offenders to reform and reintegrate into our society.
As small groups, we provided support for both offenders
and for those that were harmed in order to continue as a
functioning group.

What changed, when did we decide we could do without each other? Why…why did we make that decision and what has it cost us…what will it cost us? How did we institutionalize a tolerance for exclusion, a tolerance for abandonment and a diminishing of our human connections? To deny each other, to abandon our own dignity, our own compassion and our own humanity as we deny basic dignity to others diminishes each of us. Our collective intolerance, hatred, and maybe worst, our unconscious bias, driven by our own views of morality make the world a dangerous uncivil collection of judgmental, seemingly moral, tribes.

Do we justify that flawed morality by surrendering to a worldwide military industrial complex? Is it now a pay-to-play rationality that allows us to abandon our dignity for fellow human beings because we have the power to legislate away basic human rights? The questions that each of us needs to contemplate is how, why, when, and can we change? Can we return to a world where the sanctity of humanity can be restored? Where the dignity of life can be celebrated in our understanding, our compassion, our dignity? Can we re-embrace a sense of restorative justice, through restorative practices and find new ways to return to the old ways of knowing that we need each member of our collective tribes to reintegrate to our society and contribute to our collective humanity?

ON BEING TRUMPED OR CHUMPED

How do you restore normalcy when
you are not sure what is normal?
Can we measure normal, can we see it,
feel it, hear it, taste it, fondle it?

Is today's normal the same as
yesterday's? Will it be the same tomorrow?
I doubt it, can't prove it, might not know it anyway.
Is normal only in the eyes of the beholder and
therefore, your normal is different from my normal?

What is normal about being Trumped or Chumped?
His normal is certainly not my normal. His reality
quite possibly exists only in his mind, but the collateral
damage from his normalcy disrupts an
already confused world, bringing more
questions, less certainty, and more anxiety. But
even the bizarre becomes normal
if you are forced to live it long enough. Once
lived it is hard to change because it has become
the new normal.

ON WORKPLACE INCIVILITY

Demoralizing, demeaning, unnecessary and destructive.
No wonder 74 percent of American workers report being
disengaged at work. Absenteeism, presenteeism,
low morale, high turnover, and anemic productivity.
27 percent of workers would be willing to
sell their company data systems logins and passwords.
And sell at what price? One-third
would settle for as little as $100. Is this the casualty of
disengagement or the revenge of incivility?

What of the worker casualties as a direct
result of a toxic culture? Stress related health issues
including insomnia, clinical depression, eating disorders,
heart disease, and stomach ailments are the reward for
sucking it up and trying to survive. Enabling organizations
make these ailments commonplace as incivility
is either ignored or tolerated. Is tough management

a euphemism for a climate of incivility? What about the quality workers who escape to better options? Are they the only winners as others who cannot escape workplace injustice must simply hold on and deteriorate? Does it have to be this way, or can an uncivil environment be transformed to a productive, respectful empowering culture where great employees continue to to be great. No one hires an employee expecting them to be a disengaged failure.

The first step is to recognize the symptoms and then
search for the underlying problems generating the
abnormalities. It is not possible to legislate civility, but
learning to listen to understand, coupled with
a true belief that people are not disposable
is a good start. Restorative practices and respectful
conflict management can begin to
turn a toxic environment to a productive one.
An understanding that "conflict is not the problem,
conflict is the messenger," can begin the process.
If the message is addressed respectfully the solution
will be a workplace conflict that is positive and productive.
But, disrespectful, personally directed, hurtful,
demeaning messages most often produce toxic conflict in
the workplace. However, even that conflict can be corrected and
reversed with compassion and restorative practices.

ON UNDERSTANDING OUR WORDS

When I ask, "Would you like my advice?"
do you hear, "Let me tell you what to do"?
When I think my advice is my opinion, do you think
it is not opinion, but my way of telling you what to do?
When you do not want my advice, I think you do not
want my opinion. No wonder we both react
negatively. If we never have a conversation
about our definitions will we continue to
misunderstand each other each time I ask
if you would like my advice?

The way we independently define common words
can readily lead to ongoing miscommunication.
If we take the time to ask what we
mean by our response to the common word,
we might actually understand each other.
Is exact wording more important than exact
understanding? Is exact understanding possible
without conversation? Are exact definitions
critical to our ongoing conversations, or can
we learn to understand what we each mean?

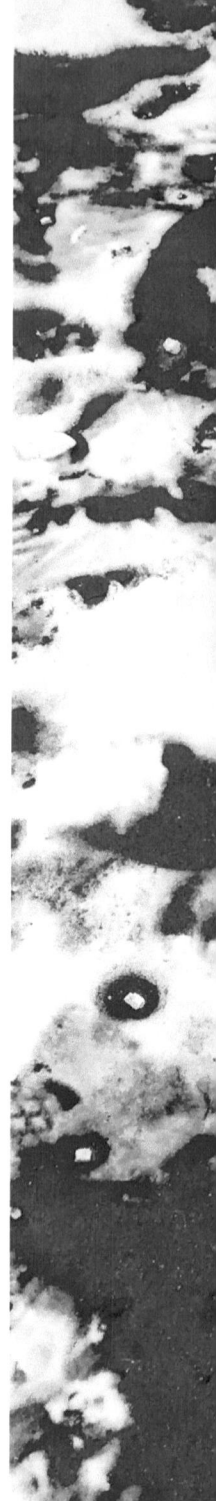

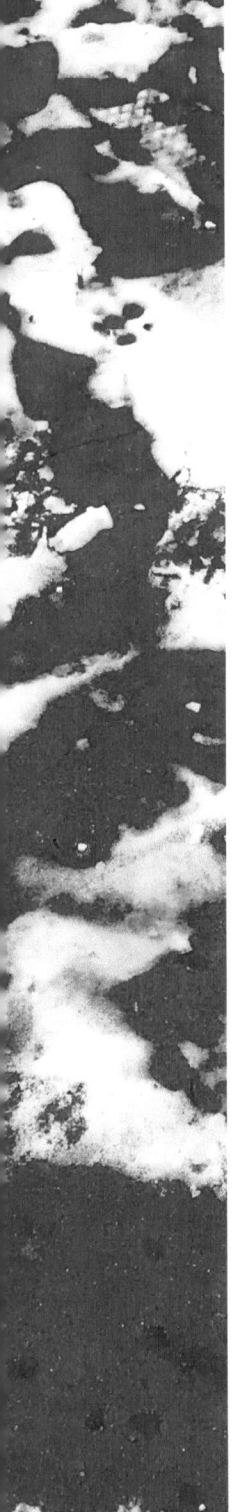

Do we wrongfully interpret and assume through
personal definitions or can we learn to understand
each other's language? Perhaps not…so, do
we need to have vocabulary discussions
to understand each other's language, or should
we ask questions of each other's statements?
Will we…or are we happy to only partially
understand each other? Is this a "failure to
communicate" as in Cool Hand Luke, or
is it our Achilles heel? Is it where our
relationship is most vulnerable?

Help me understand how we should
proceed…how we should relate…
how we should communicate. I really
want to understand you and I would
love for you to understand what I ask or say.
Otherwise we will truly have a failure to communicate.

ON TRUST, DISTRUST, AND THE SPACE BETWEEN

If someone asks you to trust them, do the opposite. Trust
cannot be requested, only earned. We earn trust by what we do
not what we say. If what we say and what we do match
you can at least trust the consistency.
If I must ask you to trust
me, am I demonstrating my own insecurity
in my words, motives,
and actions? Am I asking you to disregard your emotional
intelligence or merely suggesting you suspend it?

Do I immediately place you in the space between
trust and distrust? How long will I leave you
in that space? How old will you be when you
leave that limbo space for trust or distrust?
You will remain in that space until I can earn one
or the other. Once earned it is still fragile, still
hovering, still in play. Perhaps, my consistency
will allow you to feel more secure in your
observations.

And what of your observations, are you willing
to believe me, or your lying eyes? Maybe it `
is best that I should become a politician and therefore
subscribe to the wisdom of P.T. Barnum
"that there is one born every minute" or
W. C. Fields's famous admonishment,
"Never give a sucker an even break."
Forget your lying eyes and trust me.
I have your back, your six, I will not let
you down, and by the way, the check
is in the mail. Welcome to limbo.

ON IF YOU WANT TO KEEP IT, GIVE IT AWAY

If you want respect in your life give it away.
If you want love you must also give it away.
Compassion works exactly the same way and is only
available as a rental until you learn to give it away.

You must share each of these things if you hope to have
them regularly in your life. The act of sharing makes
each real, acceptable, and appreciated. You can
wait patiently or impatiently for respect, love, and
compassion to enter your life, or you can jumpstart
and give them away in the hope that they
will be reciprocated.
The very act of giving them away unconditionally
will allow you to keep them.

By giving them away unconditionally you can find
inner peace and contentment. You might also find that
they are returned to you in abundance. Giving them
away is the only way to find them. How could you possibly
hoard respect, love and compassion? Where would you keep
them? In what kind of vessel can they be stored?
They might just go moldy and rot in storage.
What good are they if not shared?

And in sharing you might find more
love, respect, and compassion than
you could ever imagine.

ON HOPE

Hope is our faith. It is our future, it is our North Star, it is the light at the end of the tunnel, it is the reason we persist.

Hope is the catalyst that controls our reactions, steers our ship, and helps navigate our immediate future. If we lose hope, we lose our rudder and we flounder, crash, and sink. If we are truly lucky we might find a new sense of hope and begin on a corrected course.

Our basic survival instincts will assist us to find new hope, if we are open to discovery and not wishing for closure. We must have faith in hope, for it is our future. No hope, no future.

ON THE IMPORTANCE OF FEELINGS

You may not remember the exact details,
but you will never forget how you felt
during and after it happened. Feelings create
a powerful memory that is more accurate
than the exact recall of the time and place.
Feelings are branded into our brains
and like smells, the memory resurfaces when
triggered. Survivors of trauma will never
forget how they were made to feel at the time.
Although they may confuse the time and place, they will
never forget how they felt.

Asking, "How did you feel when it happened?"
is more powerful than just asking, "Tell me what happened."
"How do you feel now?" brings back other details
of the journey of feelings and will allow the
person to recall the context. Asking the parent of an offender
how they felt when they learned their son or daughter
had done something wrong can reach to the deepest
emotions of sadness and shame.

A restorative mediation will never be complete
until all parties to the mediation have
the opportunity to explore and confront
their feelings and emotions. Good mediators
know this and will facilitate the journey. They
understand the power of feelings and know
that until addressed, repressed feelings and emotions will
undermine the long-term result of the mediation.

Think back to the time of an important event in your life,
good or bad, and try to recall the exact date, time, and
other details. Now try to remember how you felt
during and after the event.
Which memory is the most accurate?
Which emotions are the most powerful?

ON THE QUESTION OF LIFE

Life is an open-ended question. The
past can hold stories, true or not, the
future can hold promise, hope, and dreams.
Today is right now and it is reality.
No one is promised another 5 minutes.
What will you do with the present minute
you have been granted? You will use every
minute life has granted you, but how, and for what?
Do you use it with purpose, or just react
to what has happened or expect might happen?

Is converting oxygen to CO_2 your
primary purpose in life, or do you use
your respect and attention to benefit
others and therefore, have respect
and attention returned? When you ask,
"What is the meaning of life and what
is my place in the world?" do you get more
questions than answers… is this not the oldest of
human questions?

Each of us must try to answer the question
for ourselves. If it is answered for us,
do we truly believe it is our answer, or just an answer
presented by someone of authority who heeds the calling
to tell others what to think or believe.

We each need to find our own path.
Maybe, if we look to see, listen to understand,
and realize that assumptions are only assumptions,
there may be some sign posts along the way.
Like all pilgrims before us, we need to share
our stories and our questions along the path.
Our stories are what make us real, since they
contain some insights to our past, true or not.
They possibly can provide some direction to our future.

Today, right now, is where you are and it
is your story. I hope you can share it, I hope
it will be heard.

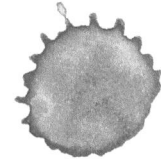

ON LEADING BY EXAMPLE

What I say is of no value, unless it matches what I do. Actions are believable, words alone are just words, with little meaning. Actions give words meaning. Body language gives words meaning. Tone and inflection give clues to the intention of my words.

Since only 7% of communication is understood through words, it is no wonder that email and texts are misunderstood, unless one adds emojis, capitalization, or the ever famous ha-ha. Without these clues the words can be readily misunderstood as wrongful assumptions and misunderstandings run rampant.

Often, we read messages through the corruption of our assumptions and our reactions and responses will exacerbate understanding and communication. Actions are different; they show intent, beliefs, and if inspirational, may demonstrate leadership.

Leadership by example is powerful, convincing, and genuine. Children are amazingly perceptive in linking and comparing words and actions. They know when words are only for effect, not for belief. Words have very little value without corresponding and matching actions. One cannot demand respect without giving respect. One cannot seek love without giving love. One cannot find hope without giving hope. Our actions are our examples and our words are meaningless without leading by example.

ON ARE YOU DISPOSABLE; ARE OTHERS?

Ancient people did not have the "luxury" of considering other people disposable. They needed everyone for the survival of the clan, family, or tribe. Members died all the time, from accidents, disease, and famine. They could not afford to treat anyone as disposable, they needed everyone for their own survival.

When did we, as human beings, begin to treat others as disposable? When did we decide we could do without whole groups of people? How arrogant and ignorant have we become to stop believing in the need for, and value of, everyone? What has this arrogance cost us; what have we lost?

The day that you decide that no one should ever be considered disposable is the day you change your thinking about everything. On that day you begin to see how foolish you and society have been in the past and how you should think about the future.

Ancient people developed a critical pathway
to survival with what we now refer
to as Restorative Justice or Restorative Practices.
They could not afford to lose a life and they found
a way for the clan to help a member who was
harmed by another member and to return normalcy.
They also found a way to reintegrate the offender
into the society in a meaningful way
through the obligation of making things right
and improved personal behavior. Some
punishment might be appropriate but not
nearly as important as the resolution of
harm and the reintegration into the society.

When we lost those lessons, we began our
journey down the slippery slope of revenge,
punishment, and ostracization. We began
the fallacy of thinking of others as disposable,
as unimportant, as less than human. What
have we lost with that thinking?

Author's Statement

This collection of poetry centers on my reflections of the concepts surrounding civility, and writing the poems has been restorative to me and to my understanding of this ancient concept.

Beginning with the traditional notion of manners and politeness (George Washington, *Rules of Civility & Decent Behavior*, 1744), and continuing to the more subtle concepts of compassion, dignity, human value, human worth, forgiveness, and self-dignity, this collection is an attempt to understand and explain a concept that has varied over time and through different cultures. The concept is often connected with civilization and civil because they share the same root word, but civility is more active, more basic, and more personal. *"Being civil to one another is much more active and positive a good than mere politeness or courtesy,"* (Robert B. Pippin, *The Persistence of Subjectivity*, 2005).

In order to fully comprehend civility, one must reevaluate the status quo and build on the ancient principles of the interdependence of human beings (Dalai Lama, *Beyond Religion*, 2011). Civility is therefore interconnected with compassion, justice and humanity.

An important research question when contemplating civility is, "When did human life become disposable, and can we reverse that belief?" As much as civility is typically associated with qualities such as politeness and the display of good manners, for contemporary social and political theorists it has increasingly come to represent civic virtues such as tolerance, non- discrimination and public reasonableness.

Civility is therefore "more" than good manners (Melanie White, An Ambivalent Civility, *Canadian Journal of Sociology*, 2006).

About the Author

John-Robert Curtin, Ph.D., is a Senior Fellow and Executive Director of the 4Civility Institute, Louisville, Kentucky and 4Civility Institute, Limited, Dublin Ireland. He is also a faculty member at the University of Louisville and at Indiana University and teaches graduate and undergraduate courses in mediation, restorative justice, and alternative dispute resolution. He is the author of An Exploratory Study of Existing State Anti-Bullying Statutes, (2016), Lambert Academic Press and a contributing author to a two-volume set, "Workplace Bullying and Mobbing" ABC-CLIO, Inc., Santa Barbara, California, January 2018. 4Civility Institute provides mediation training, ombuds training, certifications, software reporting systems, restorative justice, and behavioral transition practice solutions to schools, businesses and organizations. He has extensive experience in alternative dispute resolution, restorative justice, education, training, and in anti-bullying efforts. He is also the founder of the Connected Learning Network, an education-based company, which has provided online services to over 120 schools, colleges, businesses and organizations worldwide. In that capacity, he has been a sub-contractor to 8 European Commission funded projects and numerous U.S. funded projects. John-Robert is also known for his work in public television, as an Emmy award winning producer and station president. He has over 200 local, national and international programs to his credit. He has an Interdisciplinary Ph.D. from University of Louisville with a concentration in alternative dispute resolution. His academic background also includes creative writing and oceanography. He describes himself as a "serial social entrepreneur with an over-commitment addiction."

John-Robert began writing as an undergraduate at Syracuse University and had the great good fortune to be in Syracuse University's poetry writing program and study with Donald Justice, Phillip Booth, and W.D. Snodgrass.

About the Illustrator

Ying Kit Chan has presented his art work in over 200 exhibitions in the United States as well as in Australia, Canada, Ecuador, Germany, Korea, Japan, England, Hong Kong, Poland, Taiwan, Italy, Switzerland and Portugal. He is presently a professor of art at the University of Louisville.

Inspired by the deep ecology philosophy as well as Taoist and Buddhist ideologies, his work celebrates the richness and diversity of all life forms, and contemplates the interconnectivity and harmony of our universe.